W9-AOT-011

"*A Journey* . . . is truly a winner . . . it approaches the business world with new-found trust and courage. It reads like a short story but has organic power and relevance to the ever-changing environment in which we all compete.

The concept of the Heroic Environment is the 'Open Marriage' of business philosophy . . . it borders on organization without ego.

Very simply, your eight Heroic principles say . . . do what is right, treat others as you would expect to be treated . . . with trust and dignity. It really deals with the essence of down-to-earth values."

JIM STEVENS, Executive Vice President
and Chief Operating Officer,
Coca-Cola Enterprises

"I greatly enjoyed and appreciated your book. It cuts to the very heart of what is ailing American business today and gives some steps that can be taken to change the present course. I have since passed the book on to many others who have the same response. Thanks!"

LOREN LANDAU, Coordinator of Quality,
Texaco Refining and Marketing, Inc.

"It strikes me that the principles of the Heroic Environment and Heroic behavior are the kind of logical common sense fundamentals of life that too often get lost in big business."

ROGER D. MISSIMER, Senior Vice President,
R.R. Donnelley & Sons Co.

"Whether you're a CEO, a manager, a salesperson, or simply a dedicated employee, treat yourself to a personal journey into the Heroic Environment. For a change, see how well you can handle a big dose of good news, vital research, crystal-clear guidance, and exhilarating predictions. I hate to spoil the book by revealing the ending, but it turns out that the surest path to organizational success in the 1990s springs simply and naturally from our best instincts as good human beings. By the last page I felt as if I had climbed out of the trenches and taken a nice warm shower in the Truth. Those who own, operate, or manage any business, big or small, should make a point of reading this book—because you can rest assured that this is one business book your employees will be reading."

DANIEL W. ZADRA, Compendium, Inc.

"Over the past ten years, I've been teaching and training men and women how to build effective personal relationships. Your book is the freshest, most insightful work I've come across in a long time. It explains simply what a healthy relationship means at an organizational level."

ELLEN KREIDMAN, author of the bestselling *Light His Fire*

"Rob Lebow has created a wonderful approach to simple, age-old truths in his book, *A Journey Into the Heroic Environment*. In my opinion, Rob holds the key to organizations that will do exceptionally well in the '90s. It's must reading and must implementing."

ROBERT B. OLSON, President, the Benedictine Development Corporation

"I have recently read *A Journey Into the Heroic Environment* for the third time. I wanted to extend my thanks for sharing the message. It is stated in a simple yet effective way. The issues are extremely timely. I can't help but feel the companies that don't deal with their people in such a fashion will not survive into the next century."

RICK ELLINGSON, Vice President,
Bargreen-Ellingson Restaurant Equipment
and Design

"Henderson Homes has contracted with Heroic Environments, Inc. to help us on the Heroic Environment journey. Implementing the concepts in Rob's book is measurable in increased sales, better quality, faster response, higher profits, and, most important, more fun."

CHARLES L. HENDERSON, President,
Henderson Homes

"The Executive Committee (TEC) realizes the importance of exposing its exclusive membership of company presidents and CEOs to innovative ideas. That's why TEC embraces *A Journey Into the Heroic Environment*. It's a quality program that gets *dramatic* results."

KATHY TIGHE, Director,
Human Resources Development,
The Executive Committee

"Successful companies in the '90s and beyond will need to forge new working relationships with their employees. *A Journey Into the Heroic Environment* presents a sound approach to developing this new working relationship."

CARL BEHNKE, President,
ALPAC, Seattle

"People are our country's most valuable resource. *A Journey Into the Heroic Environment* presents very compelling concepts for organizations to create a climate for people to feel a sense of purpose.

This book will serve as a positive catalyst for organizational leaders to effectively help people to become Heroes through service."

LARRY D. CASE, Chairman,
National Council for Vocational and
Technical Education in Agriculture

A Journey Into the Heroic Environment

How to Order:

Quantity discounts are available from the publisher, Prima Publishing & Communications, P.O. Box 1260HER, Rocklin, CA 95677; telephone (916) 632-4400. On your letterhead include information concerning the intended use of the books and the number of books you wish to purchase.

For your further enjoyment, this book is available in an audio cassette. Please contact Audio Renaissance at: 5858 Wilshire Boulevard, Suite 205, Los Angeles, CA 90036; telephone (213) 939-1840.

A Journey Into the Heroic Environment

8 Principles that Lead to Greater Productivity,
Quality, Job Satisfaction, and Profits

Rob Lebow

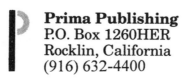

Prima Publishing
P.O. Box 1260HER
Rocklin, California
(916) 632-4400

Copyright 1990 by Heroic Environments, Inc. All Rights Reserved.
The Heroic Environments Program™ is a trademark of Heroic
Environments, Inc. The Third Generation™ of organizational development training is a trademark of Heroic Environments, Inc.
HEROIC ENVIRONMENT® is a registered trademark of Heroic
Environments, Inc. All content in this book is Copyright© pro-
tected by Heroic Environments, Inc. No part of this publication
may be reproduced, stored in a retrieval system, or transmitted, in
any form or by any means, electronic, mechanical, photocopying,
recording or otherwise, without prior permission, except for inclu-
sion of quotations in a review.

Typography by Futura Graphics
Production by Rosaleen Bertolino, Bookman Productions
Jacket design by The Dunlavey Studio

Prima Publishing

Library of Congress Cataloging-in-Publication Data

Lebow, Rob,
  A journey into the heroic environment / by Rob Lebow.
    p. cm.
  ISBN 1-55958-047-X : $16.95
  1. Job satisfaction. 2. Work environment. 3. Quality of
work life. 4. Labor productivity. I. Title.
HF5549.5.J63L43 1990
658.3'14—dc20   90-42527
                                                   CIP

94 — 10 9 8 7 6 5 4 3 2

Printed in the United States of America

Contents

A Journey Into the Heroic Environment

Chapter 1

The Journey Begins

The day was turning out to be a good one for John Spencer. He had just completed a job interview with a firm in Chicago, and things had gone well. The president of the company himself had interviewed him, and he could feel that he was being courted. This gave the young man a sense of his own importance. "Not bad, Spence," he reflected with some pride.

When John got into the cab taking him to O'Hare Airport, it was already snowing. By the time he arrived at his terminal, the snow had turned into a blizzard and his flight had been canceled. It was the holiday season, and the airport was suffocating with people. After a moment's indecision, John phoned Amtrak, booked one of the last seats available on the California Zephyr, called his wife to tell her about the change in plans, and took a taxi, which crawled to the train terminal through the blinding snow.

In spite of the hassle, John felt a guilty pleasure. He still thought of train travel as an adventure. But more important, he needed time to think.

His successful interview notwithstanding, John was still unsure of what to do. His father had worked for one company from the time he had left the army until his retirement. Yet John, in the eight years since he graduated from college, had already worked for two companies and was now considering moving to a third. Somehow, he didn't feel right about that.

It wasn't that John was not a good employee. On the contrary, at thirty-one he was already the assistant manager of the Denver plant of a large electrical component manufacturer, one of a disappearing breed still operating in the United States.

He had been rewarded well for his abilities. Yet he felt increasingly frustrated.

John felt he had been given responsibility to carry out existing policies without the ability to change them. And he wanted to make substantial changes in the way the plant operated, changes he was sure would help his firm be much more competitive. Yet the company's rigid top-down approach to decision making had made implementing new ideas almost impossible. He had to grudgingly enforce policies that he felt were working against the company's best interests.

"A train trip will give me a chance to sort all this out," John thought as he boarded the train. Compartment 417-C was two cars away, and he had to weave slowly down the passageway through the throngs of holiday travelers.

When he arrived at his semiprivate compartment, John noticed that his companion for the sixteen-hour journey was already seated comfortably, glancing out the window. John looked for a place to store his carryon. Above his companion's head was a silver rack. As John moved forward to lift his bag, the stranger turned his head and half rose, his hand instinctively stretched to support the bottom of the bag.

While taking off his overcoat and suit jacket, John glanced at his fellow passenger. He must have been in his late sixties, yet his movements exuded youthfulness. There was something reassuring about the way he smiled, which made John feel immediately at ease. He had a feeling the two of them would pass their sixteen hours together pleasantly. This instant sense of rapport surprised John since he did not easily trust others.

"Hi, I'm Stan Kiplinger, but everyone calls me Kip," the gentleman said, extending his hand, his steel-blue eyes looking straight at John, as if he were trying to read him. Those eyes revealed an astuteness and a sense of curiosity that lay just beyond their friendly twinkle. As they shook hands, John introduced himself and added, "I don't normally take the train, but it was a mess at O'Hare. Do you travel by train often?"

Kip smiled and reflected aloud that when he started in business, there was little choice but to go by train. In the mid-1950s he switched to airplanes for efficiency. Now that he had more time, he'd returned to this more leisurely mode of travel. "It gives me time to think," he added.

Kip didn't dwell long on himself. "And are you going home for the holidays?"

John nodded, "My family and I have lived in Denver for the past five years, and we really like it."

"Were you in Chicago on business . . . I hope you don't mind my asking?"

"Not at all. I was here for a job interview." John felt himself unusually eager to talk with this stranger.

"I did my fair share of that when I was your age," said Kip, nodding knowingly.

"And did you ever find what you were *really* looking for?"

With this question the older man knew that the

small talk was over, that he was being asked a serious question, one his companion was seeking an answer to. He paused a moment before responding. "It took me a long time to realize that there was no such thing as the right job. All jobs have pluses and minuses. But I learned that it is possible to find fulfillment in almost any job. In fact, I GUARANTEE that you can, too."

Although he tried not to show it, John was flabbergasted by the answer, so much so that he didn't respond for a long time. Here he was, agonizing over his career direction after two unfulfilling experiences, and this stranger was talking about job satisfaction as if it were within everyone's grasp. John's natural skepticism surfaced. "Just like that, you think I can find the perfect job?" he asked, more pointedly than he'd intended. He immediately regretted the edge in his voice.

At that moment, John and Kip were jolted as the train lurched forward to begin its journey. John stared out the window, the train's hypnotic rhythm mesmerizing him. He kept thinking about Kip's enthusiasm, which contrasted sharply with his growing cynicism. Everything in his mind kept blurring into a series of flashes: his family's reluctance to leave Denver, his most recent interview, his father's loyalty to his company, and finally, his hunger to experience a working situation that could give meaning and purpose to his life.

"I hope you're enjoying the train ride. Most people find it soothing."

Kip's voice brought John back to the present. Without replying, John abruptly asked, "Mr. Kiplinger . . . Kip, were you serious about what you said?"

"You mean about guaranteeing that you can be happy and fulfilled in your job?" He chuckled. "When I was your age I was just as frustrated and as skeptical as you."

"What changed?"

"I was lucky. During my early years I came across several key people who helped reshape my outlook. One was a man I met on a train ride . . . come to think of it, not unlike this one. I was explaining to him, with a great deal of embellishment, what was wrong with my job—why the employees were unhappy, why it was management's fault, and finally, why I deserved better. I recall now, his name was Dan Turner, and he was a sales manager for a tool and die manufacturer. Anyway, as I was speaking, his face kept getting redder by the minute until finally he blurted, 'And what are you doing to improve the working conditions of your coworkers?' I didn't know what to say—this was such an unexpected question. After all, I was just a young man at the bottom of the totem pole. What power did I have to make any difference? Mr. Turner continued, rather harshly, 'Young man, stop looking for a perfect job. Instead, help your company create a better work environment.'"

John broke in, "What did he mean by that? Did he expect you to change the working conditions and benefits?"

"No, John," Kip's voice showed impatience, as if for a moment he had become Dan Turner. "Turner believed that the secret to job satisfaction is the way you treat others and how it causes others to treat you! Over the years, I have met other key people who reinforced in me the sense that this is the right answer, that job satisfaction is almost entirely dependent on the environment that is created by individuals within the organization."

John was almost disappointed in what he heard. He had never seriously considered the working environment a factor in achieving job satisfaction. He thought all business environments were pretty much the same. He judged a job by its duties, title, power, and salary.

"I don't get it. My job isn't exciting anymore. What does that have to do with the working environment?"

A sharp knock on the door interrupted the discussion. A porter in a starched white serving jacket stuck his head in the door and asked if they wanted an afternoon snack. Kip turned to John and asked, "Would you care to join me?"

Chapter 2

Defining
the
Heroic
Environment

Once they were seated at a table in the train's dining car, John repeated his question. "I don't find my job fulfilling anymore. I feel I'm not allowed to be creative. What does this have to do with a better working environment? I don't understand."

"Look, John," Kip's voice regained its earlier warmth, "in the beginning all jobs are exciting, like a new marriage. But typically, the thrill of newness wears off and the atmosphere becomes more political. People begin to worry more about protecting their position in the organization than about excelling."

John nodded in agreement.

Kip continued, "It seems that many people have their own agendas. They blame others for their mistakes instead of taking responsibility, and they only do those things that make them look good in the eyes of management.

"But contrary to what you might think, most people *don't* want to be small-minded. They want to make a difference. They want to believe that what they do contributes to something bigger than their own self-interest—that they can be of benefit to others. It's just that most work environments, instead of fostering unselfish behavior, discourage it. Imagine what would happen in a work environment if people were given freedom to act the way they really want to act—courageously. Heroically. You can't *imagine* how happy people would be in such a place. And when people are charged up as a result of the respect and appreciation they feel, they want to contribute even more, to rise to their true potential. A Heroic Environment is a place that nurtures such a response in those who work there."

16

"Do places like that exist?" John asked.

"Yes, of course," said Kip. "True, they are all too rare, but they *do* exist."

"But how can one find such an environment?" persisted John. "Or better yet, how can someone like me help *create* such an environment?"

Kip could hardly suppress his pleasure at hearing this question. He now knew that his instincts about John's leadership qualities were not misplaced. "That's such a good question, John, that before we plunge into it, let's take a moment to refresh ourselves."

As Kip ordered a couple of soft drinks, John looked out the window. The blizzard had turned into a picturesque snowfall. A white carpet stretched as far as the eye could see, interrupted only by the pulsating rhythm of the electric poles whisking by. He could feel a new optimism swelling in his breast. If only what he was hearing were possible, he reflected, not yet ready to let go of all his doubts.

"John," Kip interrupted, "to answer your question about creating a Heroic Environment, let me first tell you where the name originates. In ancient Greece, heroes were those who acted unselfishly, who put the interests of others before their own. I am convinced that this nobility is an integral part of most human beings. Most people rise to the occasion when treated with respect, trust, and dignity.

"But to create a Heroic Environment, all individuals in the organization must agree to follow certain fundamental principles. There are only eight of them, but they are all critical. *If even one of these principles is missing, you don't have a truly Heroic Environment.*"

Kip fell silent for a moment. He realized that he was about to share with John what had taken a lifetime to learn. He could only hope that the young man would appreciate his offering.

"John, are you sure you want to hear all this?"

"Kip, you have no idea how much!"

Reassured, Kip found an extra paper napkin and started jotting down:

The Eight Principles of the Heroic Environment

1. Treat others with uncompromising truth.

2. Lavish trust on your associates.

3. Mentor unselfishly.

4. Be receptive to new ideas, regardless of their origin.

5. Take personal risks for the organization's sake.

6. Give credit where it's due.

7. Do not touch dishonest dollars.

8. Put the interests of others before your own.

John turned the napkin so he could read it more easily. It seemed a long while before he looked up. "You know, Kip, what you've written here is not new. But I have never worked in a place that practices this philosophy. Oh, sure, everyone uses the right words. But there's usually such a gap between words and deeds that no one takes them seriously. To actually put these principles to work, that *would* be something."

"Good, John," Kip answered. "You understand how important it would be to implement and use these principles. So let's get into some detail.

"The first principle of the Heroic Environment is **treat others with uncompromising truth**. What do you think that means?"

"I guess it means that everyone is told the truth all the time—that whether the news is good or bad, all the team members are informed about what's going on instead of being left in the dark, or worse, deceived."

Kip nodded. "Really, there *is* no other practical and sensible way to treat people. After all, if there's bad news, people find out anyway. Keeping the truth from teammates only causes anger and mistrust in the long run. On the other hand, telling the unvarnished truth early on brings the members of the team closer together and creates supporters instead of bystanders. And when everyone on the team is involved in solving the problem, the chances for success increase."

"I wish my company's top management practiced this principle," replied John, who was used to hearing bad news from the grapevine, not from the top.

Kip continued. "The second principle is **lavish trust on your associates.** Notice, that I'm not just saying trust people, I'm talking about trusting them and making them *feel* trusted. Do you remember the very first time someone you respected showed you how much he trusted you?"

John thought for a second. His eyes brightened with the recollection. "It was my dad. He had just brought home his new Olds. I was sixteen and had recently passed my driver's education program. Dad handed me the keys and said, 'Why don't you take her for a spin, Son?'"

"How did it feel?" asked Kip.

"On one hand, great. I felt so grown up. But on the other hand, I knew I would rather die than disappoint him. No teenager has ever driven a car more carefully."

"That's *exactly* what I'm talking about," Kip said as he half rose from his chair with enthusiasm. "When people *feel* trusted, they'll do *almost anything under the sun* not to disappoint the person who gave them the gift of trust."

John nodded with perfect understanding.

"Now let's talk about the third principle, a rather interesting one—**mentor unselfishly**. Let me tell you . . ."

"Well, this one I know something about," John interrupted. "I had a mentor in my first job. He was my boss. He was unhappy with my disorganized writing style—he couldn't understand my memos and reports. So he set aside several hours to help me and then kept monitoring and evaluating my writings. He kept doing this with me for several months until I became quite a good memo and report writer."

Kip smiled, "Good, you do understand something about mentoring. But there is much more to it. Let's take a look at the origins of the word. It is a Greek word that comes from Mentor, the loyal friend and adviser to Odysseus. You see, mentoring goes beyond teaching someone a skill. True mentoring involves teaching, advising, and befriending. Under this definition, do you currently have a mentor, and, more important, are *you yourself* mentoring anyone else?"

John shook his head.

Kip continued. "In a Heroic Environment, everyone is responsible for mentoring others."

John was puzzled. "Wait a minute. What do you mean *everyone* is responsible for mentoring? I thought that only *managers* should act as mentors to their subordinates."

"In most organizations that's the way it is. But in a Heroic Environment, people mentor unselfishly because they understand that their success depends on the success of everyone on the team.

23

"Here's an example. Let's say you are leading a convoy of ships. It is wartime, and the ships must stick together for maximum mutual protection. Most of your ships can travel at eighteen knots per hour, but two can travel at only ten knots. How fast would your convoy travel?"

"That's easy," said John, "Ten knots."

"Right. Even though you've got ships that can go much faster, you're required to slow them down to keep in formation."

"I get it," said John. "Organizations aren't much different, are they? If you have people who are lagging behind in knowledge and understanding, the whole organization slows down. The faster you can get everyone up to speed, the faster the business progresses. Isn't that right?"

Kip smiled approvingly.

"But still, isn't training the responsibility of management?"

"Theoretically, yes, of course. But there aren't

enough hours in the day for management to do it alone. Each day, there are literally hundreds of ways coworkers can help each other gain more information and understanding. In the Heroic Environment, everyone is a mentor because everyone has something to contribute. Employees also mentor their managers without fear of any negative consequences. Heroic bosses know they have much to learn from their staff."

"Okay, I think I get it," said John, looking down at the napkin. "Isn't this next remark, **be receptive to new ideas, regardless of their origin**, related to the previous principle?"

"Yes. In a Heroic Environment, ideas can spring from all corners. In fact, everyone learns to listen to new ideas regardless of their origin. No one has a monopoly on good ideas. They may come from fellow workers, vendors, consultants, articles, books, and most important, from customers. It's hard to believe, but in our fast-changing world, there are still many organizations that act as if the only good ideas come from the home office. Not only does this approach shut out good ideas, it also puts too much pressure on the managers."

"I know exactly what you're talking about," John said bitterly. "Three months ago I sent a detailed proposal to my company's home office. It took me a week of extra work at home to prepare. You know what? They didn't even bother to reply."

Kip nodded. "And how did that make you feel?"

"Rotten. In fact, that might have been the last straw that made me decide to look for another job. One thing's for sure, I won't go out of my way for them again."

"You are the perfect example of what I mean. When an organization is not receptive to new ideas, they are losing potentially vital information. Just as important, they are demoralizing their most talented, creative workers. And *when ideas are no longer proposed, the organization becomes brittle and vulnerable to market forces*. It's an organizational version of hardening of the arteries."

"The next principle really baffles me," said John. "What do you mean by **take personal risks for the organization's sake**?"

"Have you ever heard people say 'play it safe, why take a risk?' This is the attitude you find in lots of organizations, and it's the kiss of death. Risk taking is one of the most vital activities an organization must engage in if it is to survive and thrive. An organization must encourage its members to put themselves on the line by allowing them to express their ideas without fear of ridicule, or worse. This concept is important for two reasons: first, individuals need to be challenged for their own personal growth and second, an organization unwilling to look at problems from fresh perspectives is an organization unable to respond to change."

John knew what Kip was talking about. Soon after he had started his first job, he saw the career of a bright manager ruined because he championed an idea that was out of favor with his immediate bosses. The frustrating thing was that the very same idea enabled the company's leading competitor to substantially increase its market share. He also remembered the time a new employee commented on how his former company would have solved a problem. His reward was an icy stare from his supervisor and the response,

27

"Well, that's not how we do it around here." But John still had a question. "Suppose someone has an original idea, the organization implements it, and it fails?"

Kip nodded in understanding. "*Of course* it is important that the organization makes every effort to implement ideas that work. But on a controlled basis, it's essential that people be allowed to fail when they take the risk of staking a claim. Obviously, the more talented people will make more right decisions and should be rewarded accordingly. But in a Heroic Environment, people should not be attacked for failure. After all, if the organization approves the idea, it belongs to everyone."

"Isn't the next principle the other side of the coin, **give credit where it's due**?" asked John.

"In a way you're right. Many organizations don't give people a sense that they're appreciated. On the other hand, other organizations give praise so indiscriminately that it loses its meaning. Employees want to be treated like adults, not children. More than anything, they want to feel there is a rationale for praise and promotions. They want to *understand* the rewards given and *feel* that the reward and praise system is fair."

John understood all too well. "It seems as though half the promotions given by my company are questioned by the staff. Sometimes the resentments are so strong you wonder how the plant functions at all. You'd think people would be glad to see fellow employees getting rewarded."

"In a Heroic Environment, the staff understands the reason for a promotion. While they may or may not agree with it, they don't question the innate fairness behind the reward, so they aren't resentful. In fact, in a fully functioning Heroic Environment, people are genuinely happy for their successful peers."

"Kip, I'm really curious about the next principle, **do not touch dishonest dollars**. I think I know what this means, but please explain."

"Most of us think of ourselves as honest people. Yet I recently read a survey which concluded that over eighty percent of workers believe senior managers are to some degree dishonest. Obviously, there is a *perception* among employees that their leadership is not operating with full integrity, which means that employees can also rationalize not acting with total honesty themselves. The underlying problem this thinking causes is horrendous, ranging from internal theft to the leaking of vital information to a competitor. And the final result of a disregard for integrity is the disintegration of the organization's morale and self-respect.

"A company with a Heroic Environment insists that all its business transactions are assessed for their ethics, not just whether the transaction is legal, but also if it is right. That's not easy in today's world. I remember a time when people would not take unfair advantage of an opponent. Today, that is not the case. Yet of all the principles for a Heroic Environment, none is more essential."

John could feel Kip's passion welling up as he described the importance of this seventh principle. He could see some long-buried pain in Kip's eyes when he talked about the issue of integrity. But he dared not probe further. He quickly glanced down at the last principle, **put the interests of others before your own**, and said, "This sounds too good to be true."

"I won't apologize for that," said Kip, smiling. "But it is really true that when people focus their efforts on what's good for the organization as a whole rather than on their own narrow interests, everything and everyone thrives."

John sat silently for what seemed to him an eternity. Finally, he let out a low whistle. "Trying to employ all of these principles is some task, isn't it?"

"I suppose it is, John," said Kip sternly, looking at the young man with his steel-blue eyes. "But then, with all due respect to those who search for quick fixes, developing and nurturing a Heroic Environment is far too important to be trivial. What we need are people who are willing to commit themselves to the creation and sustenance of a Heroic Environment where they work. You'd be amazed what would happen to our country's revitalization if more and more organizations were run this way."

"Kip," John's voice filled with emotion, "I can promise you that I will not forget what I'm learning here."

Kip felt a rush of paternal affection toward the young man. "Well, Pilgrim," he said with his best John Wayne imitation, "I reckon there's even more for you to learn on this here cattle run."

They both burst out laughing, mostly in relief that the emotion-laden moment had passed. Walking out of the now-empty dining car, they headed back to their compartment.

Chapter 3

Walking
the
Talk

When they reached their compartment, John excused himself to stretch. The train ride reminded him of a long rail trip his family had taken when he was a teenager to visit his mother's relatives. Gradually, it all came back: the friendly people he'd met, the adventure of train travel, and the freedom he'd felt walking up and down the moving train. He stopped to stand between two cars to feel the clatter of the train wheels and the violent gyrations. A surge of raw energy went through him as the curtain of time lifted momentarily. He now remembered that on that train trip he had first kissed a girl. For a moment he was fifteen again.

But then, the magical moment passed as quickly as it had come, and his mind returned to the present. As he reviewed his extraordinary encounter with Kip, he was struck by how close he had come to settling into a mediocre corporate career. Although he had done well by most standards, he was in a rut and he knew it. He wanted his life to have meaning and purpose. Instead, for the past few years he had been coasting.

Also, he keenly felt the strong competitive winds from abroad. With his company's faltering grasp on a decreasing market share, he knew firsthand that his country's industry was in trouble. If only he could contribute by bringing new respect to the term "Made in America"—*that* would be something worth fighting for!

John's mind drifted back to his job interview. Sure, he enjoyed the warm reception he had received. But there was something too familiar with that company. He was beginning to realize that its management was not fundamentally different from the one where he presently worked. Yet somehow, it didn't make so much difference now. He was on a journey of discovery, and he felt a new optimism coursing through him. With the concepts of the Heroic Environment, perhaps he could begin to feel that his career might have meaning and purpose beyond that of simply making a living.

He hurried back to his compartment, drawn by the power of Kip's ideas. He knew he had only a few hours to master these life-changing principles, and he didn't want to waste a moment.

As he entered the compartment, he saw Kip sitting with his eyes closed, his head resting against the window. Kip opened his eyes, smiled, straightened himself up, but remained silent.

"Kip, I have a lot of questions. Do you mind if I ask them?"

"Feel free."

"How do I go about finding a company with a genuine Heroic Environment? I understand what a Heroic Environment is and I believe I would know one if I saw one, but where do I look?"

Kip thought for a moment. "Many organizations have plaques on their walls proclaiming great values: 'We believe in people,' 'Quality is our first job,' 'We're committed to innovation,' and the like. Well, don't believe these slogans until you first talk to the employees. This is called 'walking the talk.' Those who wrap themselves in lofty ideas should live by them. Unfortunately, that's not always the case. The only thing that really changes behavior is when those proclaimed values are consistently practiced at the top. Then and only then will values move down through the organization.

Kip continued. "When I was growing up, my dad used to talk to me about *Sunday values* and *everyday values*. He said, 'Kip, your Sunday values and your everyday values should be the same. Your Sunday values are important only if you intend to wear them the other six days. If not, keep your mouth shut. At least then you won't ever be called a hypocrite . . . or worse.'"

"That's pretty straight talk," said John.

"Yes, and it still applies."

"I've heard this idea also called *espoused values* versus *actual values*," replied John, "but frankly, it never made much of an impression on me before."

Kip nodded, "Over the years I've seen many disillusioned people who never recovered their trust once they understood what was behind their management's Sunday values. Preaching without integrity is explosive stuff and should be avoided. If you say one thing and do another, you'll eventually be found out.

"So to answer your question directly, the best way to check out a new company is to study how its leaders 'walk their talk.' If a company's Sunday values and everyday values are not the same, go elsewhere."

"Okay, I understand that," said John, "but doesn't a company have to develop two different sets of values: one for dealing with the outside world and one for its employees? As I study the principles of the Heroic Environment, I see that they apply primarily to the way people should treat each other *inside* the organization. What kind of values should a company develop for dealing with its customers, its suppliers, and the community at large?"

"That's a very perceptive question, John. A company needs both **external** and **internal** values." At that, Kip took some paper from his briefcase and started to draw (see Business Values chart page 41).

"Take a look at what I've written. **Business Values** are made up of a company's beliefs and actions concerning quality, customer service, environmental responsibility, community involvement, and a host of other issues. These are the external values. Of course, if you talk to twenty different companies you'll get variations on these external values, yet there'll always be fundamental areas of agreement.

"Notice that next to each of the values in the chart I left a space for both individual and company performance. That's because both the company as a whole and each employee need to examine themselves to determine if they are 'walking the talk.' Use a scale from 1 to 5 to grade your

Business Values

Directed Toward the Outside World (External)

Business Values	Your Individual Performance	Company Performance
High product quality		
Superior customer service		
High ethical business practices		
Responsible environmental policy		
Strong community involvement		
_____		
_____		

organization and yourself on how well your perfor-
mances match your values day in and day out.
Imagine what would happen if, after the company

defined its Business Values, each employee and the company as a whole graded themselves on their performance in this area."

"I understand," replied John. "I notice that you mention High Ethical Business Practices in your Business Values list. Isn't this the same as the Heroic Environment principle of not touching dishonest dollars?"

"Yes, indeed. I can only say that honesty applies both internally and externally; good ethics cannot be separated. That brings us to the next list, the People Values list." With that, Kip took a fresh sheet of paper and started sketching a new chart of People Values (please see page 43).

"Do you notice anything familiar about this list?" Kip asked, smiling.

"Sure." John looked quizzically at Kip. "It's the list of the Eight Principles of the Heroic Environment."

"Exactly. Even though a company can add additional values, the principles of the Heroic Environ-

42

People Values

Directed Toward Your Inside World (Internal)

People Performance	Your Individual Performance	Company Values
Treat others with uncompromising truth.		
Lavish trust on your associates.		
Mentor unselfishly.		
Be receptive to new ideas, regardless of their origin.		
Take personal risks for the organization's sake.		
Give credit where it's due.		
Do not touch dishonest dollars.		
Put the interests of others before your own.		
_____		
_____		

ment must be the foundation for the People Values. People Values indicate how the organization believes people inside should be treated. These values are even more important than Business Values because it is *people* who support and carry out the Business Values. If the people inside the organization don't feel they are part of a supportive environment—a Heroic Environment—they won't even bother with the Business Values.

"In filling this out, use the same process as in the Business Values chart. By grading both charts carefully, any organization and its people can diagnose precisely if they have a weakness in their internal or external values. Remember, if Sunday values and everyday values aren't the same, *if the 'walk' and the 'talk' aren't one and the same*, your company's performance will suffer, and the employees' performance will become clouded by cynicism and disillusionment."

John, ever the practical manager, still had questions. "Kip, in theory I'm sure you are right. But can you give me some examples of how all this would work in everyday business?"

Kip nodded. "John, can you think of any retail store that you absolutely refuse to buy from?"

"I can think of a couple of restaurants, as well as our nearby supermarket. The way they treat their customers . . ."

"But do you know their management, or anyone else besides the waiter or clerk you dealt with?"

"No, but just dealing with their front people was enough for me."

"That's *exactly* my point. Most customers never meet the whole organizational team. They meet a few people, say the person who answers the phone, a salesperson, a salesclerk, and so forth. From restaurants and grocery stores to hospitals, printing companies, schools, or customer service departments, the story is the same. The one person we encounter represents the whole organization to us. How we view the entire enterprise is determined by the actions of one individual. It's how this employee reflects the company's values that either attracts or repels us."

"I never thought of it that way," agreed John. "But that's so true. I judge an organization by how I'm treated, and if I'm not treated well, I won't remain a customer."

"We're all like that. And yet most organizations obviously don't understand this. Why else would they have their least skilled workers answering the phone?

"John, you asked for examples. Indulge me for awhile, as I tell you this true story. In a small town in California, a plainly dressed man, about my age, was in the process of paying his parking ticket when the attendant informed him that he could get it validated by the bank where he was a customer. Being old-fashioned enough to know the value of money, the gent returned to the bank to get his ticket stamped. After patiently standing in the bank's customer line for several minutes, he approached the next available teller and re-quested that his parking ticket be validated. She asked what transaction had taken place, as she skeptically eyed the humbly dressed man. For some reason, this teller was not in a generous mood and refused to validate the ticket.

46

"Well, the fellow was annoyed and started to raise his voice. A supervisor came running over and listened to the teller's argument. Earlier that week the supervisor had attended a company training seminar on 'Team Building' and thought he knew exactly what to do."

"I guess he stepped in and validated the man's ticket," said John.

"On the contrary. He had just learned the importance of sticking by his teammates. So he decided to support his bank clerk's decision. You see, the customer had only used the automatic teller machine outside to make a deposit. In the opinion of the clerk, this was technically not a 'bank transaction.'

"The customer quietly inquired if a withdrawal would be considered a bank transaction. 'Certainly,' said the supervisor, at which point the customer withdrew his entire account to the tune of $2,150,000. Smiling, the gentleman politely asked the speechless supervisor to validate his ticket. He then proceeded across the street to a competing bank, where he deposited the entire amount.

47

"Here is the lesson to be learned. When you don't have your People Values and Business Values in balance and universally adopted by everyone, you are often influenced by training programs and company policies that may be well-meaning but don't serve your customers and employees well. And, as in this case, when you add the additional sin of judging people by their appearance, you have the recipe for disaster.

"The treatment of people is learned behavior. If the people we work for and with treat us with respect, then we, in turn, will be likely to continue this behavior pattern. That's why organizations have personalities of their own. In a Heroic Environment, every employee is taught to respect others . . ."

"No, Kip," interrupted John. "They don't have to be taught to respect others because in the Heroic Environment they learn that from the way they are treated."

Kip smiled the smile of a teacher who knows that his lesson is getting through. He continued, "There are many well-meaning companies that are putting together customer service and quality assurance programs. It seems to me that it would be a lot better if companies *really* understood how simple the problems are. Introducing these programs *will not produce lasting results unless you first have the proper environment in place.*"

Kip looked at his pocketwatch after seeing that it had long since turned dark. "Why don't we get something to eat before we talk ourselves out of dinner?" he asked.

John was still deep in thought. Each time he felt he understood the full significance of the Heroic Environment he was introduced to more thought-provoking ideas. He saw clearly that the Heroic Environment is no "pie in the sky" for creating fulfilling working conditions. Rather, it is a core idea on which revolves the successful future of any organization.

As he got up to join Kip for dinner, his mind went back to the story of the old man and the bank. He wondered how Kip was so intimately familiar with what had happened. And then, he understood. . . .

49

Chapter 4

Understanding
Heroic
Behavior

John would not remember his dinner that evening. He felt eager to start implementing the concepts of the Heroic Environment, but he had one overriding problem he could not solve. Kip, on the other hand, seemed to be enjoying every morsel of his pot roast. He joked with the waiter as if they were old friends, and he kept the conversation light, deflecting John's attempts to return to their ongoing discussion.

Finally, Kip put his fork down, emptied his glass of water, and folded his napkin on the table. "John, you look perplexed, what is it?"

"Kip, I'm overwhelmed. I would like to institute the principles of the Heroic Environment where I work, but how do I get started? I mean, they're great building blocks if the whole organization implements them. But how does someone like me, who is not the company's president or even the plant manager, start instituting change within an organization that hasn't agreed to act heroically? I feel as though I've been given a blueprint without a set of instructions."

Kip nodded. "You're right, of course. The Heroic Environment cannot be instituted until management and staff are committed to it. But in the meantime, there is a way to begin on a more modest, individual level. You can start with the group of employees you are directly responsible for, whether they number one or fifty. You first have to build a basic level of agreement among this small group, and it has to do with the way you treat them and the way they respond in kind.

"There are five individual behavior traits involved. Together, I call these five traits Heroic *Behavior*." Kip turned his place mat over and quickly penned the five traits:

Heroic Behavior

1. Give and receive permission to act with autonomy.

2. Treat others as significant.

3. Make everyone feel like an insider.

4. Trust.

5. Act with integrity.

John studied the paper. "So starting with Heroic Behavior can eventually lead to the creation of the Heroic Environment."

"Yes. It's a modest way of beginning now, of blooming where you're planted. What eventually happens is that when you put Heroic Behavior to action in your office or department, you start a process that eventually gets noticed. And that's how it all begins.

"But let's talk about the first trait, **give and**

receive permission to act with autonomy," said Kip. "It's amazing how many managers tend to overmanage their employees. They don't seem to realize that by constantly hovering over their staff they are suffocating their employees' creativity and sense of adulthood. This becomes a self-fulfilling prophecy. When people are not given the chance to act responsibly, out of their own choice, they don't—they act like children. Furthermore, overbearing managers kill the sense of creativity that lies in most individuals."

"Okay, okay," John jumped in, feeling acutely uncomfortable, "to some extent you are describing me. I know that I tend to overmanage. But if I don't watch what my people are doing, how can I be responsible for the results?"

"I understand," Kip smiled sympathetically. "A good manager, like a good coach, has three tasks that must be done well. First, the manager must make sure that the team is good. Second, the manager should give the team a clear idea of the desired results. And lastly, the manager should give team members as much freedom as possible to succeed. Only in the case of failure should the manager ever consider reducing a team member's autonomy. Even then, as soon as the employee performs well again, autonomy should be restored; otherwise, the employee doesn't belong on the team."

"Wow," John whispered, "it's so simple, isn't it? Why do we tend to make things so complicated?"

"John, overmanaged employees are like ships with ten years growth of barnacles on the bottom of their hulls—they create unnecessary resistance and inefficiency. In the Heroic Environment, self-management is encouraged, and responsibility is delegated downward," said Kip. "The results are a lot better, and the company grows faster. I once heard someone say, 'You can lead a thousand people, but you can't carry even three on your back.'"

"It would be amusing, if it didn't hit home so hard," said John, shaking his head.

Kip continued. "The second trait is **treat others as significant**. People need to feel special and valued. What this means is that everyone in the work group is empowered with a sense of importance. Furthermore, they are also taught how to show appreciation to fellow workers. To instill this behavior is quite easy. It simply has to start with you. You'll be amazed how quickly everyone catches on.

"This brings me to an interesting survey you may have heard about. Not long ago, the U.S. Chamber of Commerce conducted a study on what employees want. They proceeded to show both employees and managers ten priorities and asked them to rate them from 1 to 10, with 1 being the most important. Let me show you the results." Kip reached into his coat pocket and removed a folded piece of paper (see page 59).

"Notice how far apart employees and managers are from each other."

John let out a low whistle. "Why is that?"

"Perhaps it's because our managers are taught principles that no longer apply today. The reason employees don't put good wages as their number one priority is that they take a decent wage for granted—we are no longer working in sweatshops.

What Do Employees Want?

Items Rated by Employees and Employers	Rating by Employees (in order of importance)	Rating by Management (in order of importance)
1. Appreciation	1	8
2. Feeling "in" on things	2	10
3. Help on personal problems	3	9
4. Job Security	4	2
5. Good wages	5	1
6. Interesting work	6	5
7. Promotions	7	3
8. Management loyalty to workers	8	6
9. Good working conditions	9	4
10. Tactful disciplining	10	7

Source: U.S. Chamber of Commerce © 1986. *The Balanced Program.*

59

The new breed of employees are looking for more than good wages; they're seeking to be part of an extended family of productive people, where everyone matters.

"Even today, you still hear some managers say, 'If so and so doesn't like it here, let him go elsewhere.' What foolish arrogance! Good employees are a company's most important asset. In a Heroic Environment there is no us/them mentality. Hierarchies are deemphasized. Everyone uses the term 'we' when talking about the company.

"This leads me to the third trait of Heroic Behavior: **make everyone feel like an insider**. People need to feel that they belong, that they have 'insider' status in their workplace. Otherwise, they feel alienated."

"I'm not sure I have a handle on how this works," said John.

Kip thought for a moment. "Okay, here's a good example of how *not* to treat people. In the 1970s and early 80s, as Detroit was seeing its market share eroding quickly to foreign car manufactur-

60

ers, panic set in, with everyone blaming others for the problem. One plant manager decided that the problem was one of image. So he issued a memo forbidding those employees not driving a company-manufactured car from parking in the salaried employees' and guests' parking lot. 'This condition does not convey a positive image to other salaried employees or guests who visit our plant,' the memo stated, 'and it has a negative impact on our share of the car market. Henceforth, salaried workers driving the offending cars will be banished to the hourly workers' lot.'

"Now, as you know, the hourly workers are generally the assembly workers—people with more direct contact with making cars than the secretaries, managers, accountants, and other salaried staff. And they were offended. Here's what the vice president of the local union said: 'They're punishing the salaried employees by telling them to park with my people, as if *we* were dogs. A lot of us consider this offensive.'"

"I bet the union had a field day with this one!" John exclaimed gleefully.

"Frankly, that's not the point. The point is that here the plant's most important asset, the people who build its cars, were treated like outsiders by an unthinking manager. It's not as if they weren't concerned about the company's problems—over a third of their friends had already lost their jobs.

"John, nobody likes to feel like a second-class citizen. I believe that people want to be part of building something important. And they want to be 'in' on decisions. That's why smart managers bring their people together to discuss problems. Often, it is the hands-on people who have the solution. *Involve employees in finding solutions and you have unleashed an invaluable resource.*"

"I think there's another way employees are left outside," added John. "In my company, I see new employees given very little instruction, and then their managers wait for them to make a mistake, which is then corrected. It's almost like the fraternity ritual of hazing: Make the task as hard as possible, and see who survives."

"Yes, it's a form of withholding information, and most non-Heroic companies practice it. It's often not a conscious act, just a relic of a more oppressive past. Mentoring people from the very beginning is so important. Teach them the ropes properly, and you'll find yourself doing a lot of praising instead of criticizing.

"John, there's a saying that information is power. Many try to withhold it, believing that by doing so they become more powerful. Ironically, the reverse is true. The most powerful people throughout the ages were the men and women who *freely* gave of their knowledge. In fact, in our information age, the more information you can share with more people, the more powerful you and your group become."

John sat silently. Some of what he was hearing was painful because it revealed his failings. He had always considered himself a good manager; now he wasn't so sure. Finally, he said, "I never realized before to what extent what I *am* affects everyone who works for me. What a responsibility!"

Kip smiled, "Well, I have something that will cheer you up."

He motioned to the waiter and ordered them both a strawberry shortcake. "It's not exactly on my diet, but our minds have been working overtime, so let's splurge a little." Listening to Kip's cheerful talk helped John relax. He realized how important it was for him to earn Kip's respect. And Kip's nonjudgmental attitude toward him was a lesson in mentoring all by itself. As their dessert was served, both John and Kip took the opportunity to enjoy the punctuated silence of the rumbling train. There was something soothing about the distant cacophony of steel rolling over iron.

Finally, Kip settled back in his seat and began discussing the fourth trait of Heroic Behavior. "**Trust** acts as an empowering message to others. In an atmosphere thick with suspicion, everyone is afraid to react spontaneously. As a result, the organization becomes inflexible and brittle. It cannot adjust quickly to change.

"Trust, on the other hand, is the damndest thing. It is hard to define, and so many people talk about it, yet few know how to extend it. I think that's because trust is the most Heroic of all traits.

You really have to overcome the fear of having your trust betrayed to risk trusting others. It's a little like jumping into the darkness with the confidence that someone will be there to catch you— and that's Heroic. Is it worth it? Absolutely, because a team that trusts its members will always out-achieve a team that is ruled by distrust and intimidation. Unfortunately, most organizations try to get results from people by manipulating them instead of trusting them."

"Why is that?" asked John.

"It goes back to a different belief system about managing people. In the early sixties the buzz word was 'Management by Objectives.' This was a concept about how to delegate tasks and achieve results, and people got all excited about it. By people, I really mean senior managers, many of whom had been military officers and who were comfortable with wielding power and having control. So of course they got excited about a system that gave them a measurable way to control the people below them. Kind of a foolproof accountability system. The only problem was, this widely accepted technique didn't take into consideration how people really *want* to be treated and how they perform best.

"The next thing we knew, everyone was delegating and managing by objectives, but no one was extending or lavishing trust. Instead, they were controlling and acting like cops. And to make matters worse, the system included penalties for failure, all without any input from the poor devils who had to live under this 'great, new, modern system.' At that point, we had entered the era of hermetically sealed management," said Kip, smiling sadly. "In a tragic way, people were losing faith in each other.

"The major problem with all this is that we were imposing on people systems they had no control over. Crunching numbers and hitting abstract goals became all important. Some 'experts' actually believed that since robots would eventually take over factory tasks, there was no reason to be concerned about people issues. You can pretty much trace America's competitive decline to that time."

"I understand," responded John. "But surely, we

do need standards. How do we achieve them without controlling people?"

"By developing responsibility throughout the entire organization. That way, people at all levels take on the role of quality control. And all the evidence shows that with few exceptions, people who have been extended trust will naturally respond to new and higher standards of quality, ethical behavior, fairness, personal autonomy, and creativity," said Kip.

John felt elated. "I've got it. It's so simple."

"Perhaps, but it isn't *easy.* It's not just that managers who have decided not to be 'cops' have to reorient their thinking. Employees who were treated like objects have to release their own defense mechanisms. It doesn't happen overnight."

"How do you know when you're succeeding?"

"One way is when you start hearing over and over from job applicants that they have heard about the great working conditions—and that they heard about it from your employees! That's when you know your team members are acting as the company's ambassadors.

"Now, the fifth trait of Heroic Behavior is just as important: **act with integrity**," said Kip.

"I hear that word so often I no longer know what it means. What's *your* definition?" asked John.

"Integrity deals with the most far-reaching question of all. It constantly asks the critical question: What does our office, our group, or our organization stand for?"

John looked perplexed.

"Let me tell you a story that will explain this," said Kip. "Not long ago, the CEO of a company and a group of his senior managers were all together in a product-planning meeting. The topic was the shipping date of a new product the company had been working on for two years. There was a pile of purchase orders waiting to be filled, and articles about the product had been written in industry magazines. Industrywide anticipation was high. Furthermore, with all the advance orders, if the product could be shipped by the end of the quarter, the company would reach the sales and profit figures it had promised Wall Street, and the CEO would be the darling of his board of directors.

"But there was a problem. The head of product development said there were glitches with the product and it would not be ready for shipment by the end of the quarter. The CEO hit the roof. Something had to be done! In his best Management by Objectives style he asked what other product could be shipped instead. The head of product development said there was an earlier version of the product that had several unsolved bugs but which could be resurrected. That was the only alternative."

"So what happened?" asked John.

"The CEO ordered the old prototype be shipped instead."

"But why?"

"So that they could meet their financial numbers for the blasted quarter. Now the story really heats up. When production heard that the defective product was going to be shipped, they couldn't believe their ears. Quality control put up a big stink, customer support started to gear up for an avalanche of problems, and the sales department found themselves caught up between loyalty to their company and loyalty to their customers. Now let's see what happened as a result.

"Because production felt the product was inferior, they spent all their efforts disavowing any responsibility. Quality control followed suit because they felt their concerns were overridden and because they were embarrassed by the whole affair.

"Customer support was outraged. They felt victimized in a war between unhappy customers and their company. And sales, after initial elation that their back orders would be filled, realized that what they were selling would damage their relationship with their clients for a long time."

"I can't believe all these problems weren't seen

before this decision was made," John said.

"Oh, there's more," said Kip. "Public relations was the last to find out about this. They were in a bind. Should they deny the allegations about a shoddy product, or should they admit the problem? If they admitted the faults, they would have to answer to the public and press why the product was released in the first place. Or, if they denied the problem, they would risk personal and professional loss of reputation in the future. Not only that, if they coordinated their answers with other corporate departments, they could even be accused of willful wrongdoing and illegal conspiracy.

"Well, John, as you can see, one decision at the highest level to achieve some numerical goals was costing this organization its integrity, its soul. Instead of heroically telling the truth by announcing to everyone that the product would be shipping late, the company squandered the trust of its employees, vendors, and the public.

"People need to be part of something they can feel proud of," Kip said with special emphasis.

71

"No wonder so many employees perceive senior management as being dishonest and incompetent," exclaimed the young man.

"John, remember this well. When it comes to integrity, there are no shortcuts. As you rise up the ranks, as I'm sure you will, there will be times when the pressure will be on you to perform, to achieve a goal, and you'll be tempted to take a shortcut. When that time comes, remember this moment, and do the right thing.

"But let me apply this behavior to your situation today. Suppose you are enacting Heroic Behavior with your group, and your company asks you to do something that you consider unethical; would you do it?"

John thought for a long while. "First, I would have to be certain in my mind that the order is really unethical, as opposed to one I disagree with. After all, as a member of the corporate team, I must execute many decisions I may not agree with. However, if, after much soul-searching, I could be certain it was a matter of ethics, I would use every available channel to voice my objections to my superiors."

"And risk your chances for advancement, even your job?"

"Yes."

"Suppose they ignore your opposition?" pressed Kip.

"Then I would have no choice but to resign."

"You mean you would risk losing everything you've worked for for the sake of your integrity?"

"Everything I've worked for would be worth *nothing* without my integrity," John replied with special emphasis.

There was silence for what seemed like a long time.

The waiter stopped by the table with a coffee-pot and the check. Kip asked when the train would arrive at the Kansas City station. The waiter looked at his watch and said they were due to arrive in two hours, around 11:00 P.M. Kip explained that the next shift would take over then and that a friend of his would be the new engineer. "Her name is Peggy Bentley. Her father and I go back a long way. In fact, I'm Peggy's godfather. When we get to the station I'd like you to meet her."

Chapter 5

The Four Corporate Personality Traits

As the two men returned to their compartment, John reached for his briefcase and wrote some notes about their dinner conversation. He wanted to make sure he wouldn't forget what he was learning. The five steps toward Heroic Behavior struck both an emotional and a rational chord, and it made sense that developing this kind of behavior would be a good first step toward creating a Heroic Environment. Yet even as he was writing, new questions were begging to be answered.

"Kip, I'm afraid you aren't quite rid of me . . . do you mind?"

"Not at all," said Kip, putting down his newspaper, "I'm just surprised you don't want to take a break from all this."

"I can't," the young man blurted out. Then, as he realized how intense he'd sounded, he smiled self-consciously. Kip returned his smile, and John relaxed.

"Okay, I now understand Heroic Behavior. Heroic Behavior creates an atmosphere where people can act Heroically, doesn't it?"

Kip nodded.

"Then would you please define for me your ideal definition of a Hero?"

"Let me start by telling you about someone I admired very much. I once worked with Max, a very special man. He developed an uncanny ability to cut right to the heart of a problem by understanding the human factors behind it. And when he would resolve a problem, he would do it with everyone's ego intact. He seemed to know exactly how to treat others.

78

"Max had a gift for understanding human needs. He reinforced his coworkers' sense of self-esteem without coming off as insincere. He made everyone feel important. Even if he disagreed with someone, that person would walk away from him feeling more focused and inspired. He knew how to keep the discussion on the issues, never attacking a person's sense of dignity in the process.

"At the time I was working with him, I was young and worked long hours. I thought pretty highly of myself. And yet I wasn't getting half the bottom-line results Max was. One day, utterly frustrated, I cornered him and asked directly about his success. His answer was simple, 'Kip, I put the needs of others before my own.'

"Frankly, I didn't buy it—his answer seemed far too simplistic. I dismissed his words, but I couldn't dismiss his ongoing success. I saw how his influence grew without his seeming to work at it. So I started to take more notice, and you know what? Max was right. It *was* his genuine interest in others and how others responded to him that made the difference.

"He had other virtues. He would stand up for the things and the people he believed in without fear or favor. When necessary, he would take charge, yet he much preferred to let his employees try their hand at leadership. At such times he would roll up his sleeves and become just one of the team members. As a result, those around him became experienced and confident leaders themselves. And, of course, by developing a team of capable, enthusiastic people, Max was now using minimal time supervising and maximum time creating and producing. Where I was spending sixty percent of my time making sure my team got the job done, he was spending only ten percent—and getting better results.

"John, you should have seen his genuine happiness when he saw his coworkers succeeding. He was so optimistic. Yet he wasn't the least bit naive. He could smell a phoney a mile away, and he would turn off immediately."

"So *that's* your model for the Hero," exclaimed John.

"Guilty as charged," Kip answered good-naturedly. "But let's generalize our discussion so that it can apply anywhere.

"Heroes make things happen. They are the men and women who tend to focus on finding solutions while others are still defining the problem. They are results-oriented, not process-oriented. And because of their 'can do' attitude, they move the whole organization forward. A Hero's motto is, 'It doesn't matter who gets the credit as long as the job gets done.' And because they are *results*-driven, not *ego*-driven, they tend to throw the limelight on others. Yet, paradoxically, Heroes become immensely powerful in a positive way. Why? Because their motives are universally trusted.

"Heroes are also facilitators of new ideas. When they discover a beneficial idea, they champion it, regardless of its source. And then they fight for its success by working toward reaching a consensus.

"The most important value of Heroes is that they create a model of behavior for others to emulate. They bring out the best in people and, as such, define the direction of the team."

81

As Kip was talking, he noticed a crestfallen look on John's face. He seemed distracted and fidgety. "What's wrong, John?" he asked, concerned.

John looked at Kip, shaking his head, "The more you describe the Hero, the less confident I am that I could be like that. Look," he said with an edge in his voice, " I try to put the interests of others before my own, but I don't always succeed. Nor do I often stand up for unpopular ideas in meetings, even if I agree with them . . . I haven't always acted courageously."

Kip understood. "John, acting Heroically is a process. None of us succeeds all the time, but it's a model for which we strive. And when we stray from it we can return to it."

"Okay, I can accept that," John answered. "But there's another question that's been bothering me. Can you honestly expect every member of the Heroic Environment to become a Hero in the way you just defined? What about the differences in personalities, capabilities, capacity, and even *commitment*? Do you really believe that all people see themselves as Heroes?"

Kip nodded, smiling, "You force me to get into more depth than I thought I'd need to," fully enjoying his young friend's display of honesty and keen mind. "You are absolutely right. There are different personality traits as well as different levels of capacity, commitment, and courage. The old saying that 'it takes all types to make the world go round' still applies. Let me first explain what I mean by personality traits.

"Most experts agree that our personality is a result of our genetic makeup and our past experiences, especially childhood experiences. Our personality emerges as we try to make our way in this world. Some of us learn that it is more pleasant to be liked and accepted, even if it means being like everyone else. Others feel compelled to become leaders and be admired. Yet others learn that their different way of seeing the world makes them unpopular. I believe that today kids call this type of person a 'Nerd.'

"So you see, John," Kip continued, "it's important to not *judge* people for being who they are. By the time they come into contact with you in the workplace, they have developed a set of behavior patterns that helps form their basic personality. I call this the person's **Dominant Trait**.

"Over the years I've found it extremely useful to think in terms of four **Dominant Traits** interacting in an organization: the **Hero**, the **Maverick**, the **9 to 5er**, and the **Dissident**.

"I've already described my idea of the Hero, so let me tell you about the **Maverick**. Mavericks are noted for coming up with new ideas, methods, and strategies. Their ideas keep an organization or group competitive and challenged. They are the original thinkers—the poets. They represent our creative best—what we can become if we allow ourselves to dream and imagine.

"Mavericks deal with the world in two ways. Either they welcome controversy, as they flaunt their disregard for what others think—I'm sure you can think of some performers and artists as well as entrepreneurs who might fall into this category—or, as happens *much* more often, they are the poets, the dreamers, the philosophers, the scientists, and the thinkers—people who often withdraw into their own world. These creative types have learned to live without group acceptance. They are in the habit of developing new ideas on their own. Because society has always treated them as 'different,' they are generally mistrustful and have poor communications skills.

"Mavericks are some of my favorite people. Most of us believe that old saying, 'If it ain't broke, don't fix it,' until our competition leaves us in the dust. Mavericks keep us on our toes by insisting that just because it 'ain't broke' doesn't mean we shouldn't try to make it better. Of course, no one likes to hear this, so Mavericks often end up in hot water because some in power interpret new ideas or disagreements as a challenge to their leadership. How unfortunate!

"The truth is, when an organization is in crisis, it will probably be a Maverick who will bail it out with an original solution. So when an organization listens to its Mavericks, it safeguards against corporate failure and ensures long-term success." Kip's emphatic tone told John that his mentor was speaking from personal experience.

John wanted to make sure he understood the

Maverick. "Are Mavericks, then, the complainers —the people who play devil's advocate?"

"Not at all. They are independent thinkers who may see a different solution from the rest of the group. For them the issue isn't dissent. Because they have vision, they look to more far-reaching solutions to problems than the majority. If they have to complain or play devil's advocate, they will, but for them the only issue is getting the best results possible."

"Does that mean that we must always accept the opinion of Mavericks?" asked John.

"Of course not. Mavericks often come up with highly impractical ideas. The key is to learn to listen with an open mind before judging the merit of an idea. Furthermore, it's important to recognize how much courage it takes to be a Maverick."

"Courage? Why courage?" asked John.

"Have you ever stood up and offered an opinion at a meeting?" asked Kip.

86

"Sure, but I was always uncomfortable until I saw how people responded to it."

"Meaning that if your idea was liked, you relaxed again?"

John nodded.

"Now, imagine spending your life offering proposals and ideas that are frequently rejected. If you have the guts to get up again and again and propose new ideas, don't you think you would be courageous?"

"I see your point, Kip."

"Alright, now that we understand the Dominant Trait of a Maverick, let's discuss the **9 to 5er**."

John smiled a slightly disparaging smile, which did not escape Kip's notice.

"Because of the term I use for them, you might think I don't respect 9 to 5ers," he said, eyeing John intently. "Nothing could be further from the truth. The historian Will Durant explains it best. He says the story of humankind is like a river. The major personalities and events are like torrents that sweep everything in their wake. But on the banks of the river are the villagers who live their lives, raise their families, grow their food, regardless of what Heroic or terrible events occur around them.

"Think of the 9 to 5ers as these villagers. They are involved in building a better life for themselves and their families. While they're at work, they work. And if you give them good instructions and treat them with respect, they'll do a good job.

"But for them, work is not everything. They balance their life between work and play. They are devoted parents, and they have a strong sense of community. But if you ever need them, they'll go the extra mile for you, as long as you treat them with the respect they deserve.

"9 to 5ers are also the most influenced by their working environment. They can be either motivated or apathetic—it all depends on the way they are treated. It also takes courage to be a 9 to 5er."

John wasn't convinced. "Why would you call 9 to 5ers courageous?"

"Let me answer you with a little story. Not long ago I sat by a young woman on an airplane. Her name was Cynthia. Her company was sending her for a computer course to learn new skills in her area—inventory control. I asked her about her job and her life. She told me she was divorced with two young children. She was a devoted mother who was frustrated because she didn't always have the time she wanted for the kids, but she did her best. She also held a full-time job she had to commute to over an hour each way and for which she had just received a promotion. In addition, she was going to school one night a week. And yet here she was, willing to learn new skills to help her company do better. Now I ask you, is Cynthia courageous?"

"I see what you mean. Like the unsung Heroes of wartime, 9 to 5ers are the unsung Heroes of the workplace," John said with a new sense of respect.

"Now you understand!" Kip said with emphasis. "9 to 5ers may not set the world on fire with their leadership or creativity, but day in and day out, they carry on the work they are assigned. Without them the organization would sputter and come to a halt."

John remained silent for awhile. He was beginning to realize that deep respect for all people is the foundation for the Heroic Environment. He remembered recent incidents where he might have been abrupt with some of his plant workers, and he felt inwardly embarrassed. He resolved to not let that happen again.

Finally, his attention returned to his conversation with Kip.

"Tell me about the last personality trait—the **Dissident**."

"Ah, yes, the Dissident . . . he is an integral part of almost every organization," Kip said thoughtfully. "But before I talk about the Dissident, I'd like to make three points. First, unlike the other Dominant Traits, which are a part of people's basic makeup, Dissident behavior is often created by circumstances at the workplace. Second, this behavior is the only one of the four that is essentially negative. Third, and most important, I want to make sure you understand that Dissident Behavior is not the same as dissenting opinion. In the Heroic Environment, dissenting opinions are actively encouraged, even sought after. An honest difference of opinion is vital to the survival and success of any organization. The key to honest dissent is that the disagreement comes out of a genuine desire to help the group achieve its goals. On the other hand, Dissident Behavior, as I define it here, happens when a person no longer roots for the team's success."

"Why wouldn't someone want to see his own team win?" asked John.

"There are several reasons. A Dissident could be a former Maverick whose proposal was rejected for someone else's and who now is hoping that the accepted proposal will fail. Or he could be a 9 to 5er who feels that his leaders are not 'walking the talk' and is therefore bitter. The Dissident could be a fallen Hero who cannot accept the authority of another leader . . ."

"I see," interrupted John. "People who no longer see themselves as *part* of the team often become the Dissidents."

"That's it in a nutshell!" said Kip, impressed with John's insight.

"Then what we must do as soon as we see Dissident behavior is help that person feel once again part of the team," continued John, taking over the discussion. "It all goes back to the Heroic Behavior of helping people feel like insiders, doesn't it?"

Kip nodded.

"The way I see it," John continued, "we all feel outside the team sometimes. The worst possible thing to do would be to isolate the Dissident further."

"Well done, John. You're on the right track. The best way to help Dissidents is to embrace them and bring them back on board. Of course, this doesn't always work. Ultimately, Dissidents themselves must recognize their own counterproductive behavior."

John seemed perplexed, so Kip continued.

"Let me tell you this true story to illustrate what I mean.

Two partners, Alan and Peter, who together had built an advertising agency, were at a point where their differences had begun to destroy their relationship. In the early years they were inseparable and their business had grown and prospered. They genuinely liked and enjoyed each other. Often, in the middle of a sales presentation, one would finish the other's sentence. But with the passage of time that all changed. Both men came to dwell upon the other's shortcomings, missed opportunities, blind spots, and vulnerabilities. Instead of acting Heroically and putting the other's interest first, their bickering turned ugly. In fact, they communicated with each other mostly through their administrative assistants, who nicknamed the situation 'the Cold War.'

"Alan was the older of the two and served as head copywriter for the agency. He had a sharp wit, was a natty dresser, and demanded perfection from his staff. Peter, a free spirit, was the creative art director. His suits never seemed to be pressed and his style was imprecise. But his employees and clients loved him for his spontaneity and gift for design. Each man's strengths matched the other's weaknesses.

"Because of their Cold War, the entire agency suffered. Employees were actively taking sides, with the popular Peter definitely winning the loyalty of the team. Alan was feeling increasingly isolated at his own agency.

"One day the agency was invited to present its work to a major potential client who had been on their dream list for years. Here was their big chance, and it couldn't have happened at a more critical time. Their Cold War had taken its toll, and the company was on its last legs financially. Getting this account could save their agency.

"As is sometimes the case with busy clients, they were asked to give their presentation on the weekend. Peter insisted on driving. Alan relented, uneasily, even though Peter was known to run late. The presentation was to be held in New Jersey, and Peter promised to pick Alan up at his

New York City apartment at 10:30 A.M. sharp, giving them plenty of time to arrive at their noon presentation.

"Alan was downstairs at the curb ten minutes early just to make sure; 10:30 came, no Peter. By 10:45 Alan was upset. By 11:00 he was contemplating murder.

"Finally, at 11:10, Peter pulled up, completely unruffled at being forty minutes late. Alan, losing every vestige of self-control and feeling sorry for himself, started screaming at Peter, 'You've made us miss the presentation! I knew I shouldn't have trusted you! Now we'll never make it on time.'

"Peter calmly turned to Alan and said, 'Don't worry, I've got a shortcut!'

'A what?' shrieked Alan. 'A shortcut,' said Peter. 'In fact, that's why I'm late—I was getting the directions. This shortcut will chop nearly twenty-five minutes from the ride, so we have plenty of time.'

"As he entered the car, Alan was still bristling. For once, he wanted Peter to get his comeuppance.

Suddenly, he had a realization. 'Good Heavens, what am I hoping for?' he thought. 'Am I hoping Peter's shortcut will work and get us there on time so we can get the account, or am I hoping he'll fail in order to reinforce my belief that Peter is a fool who's responsible for all our problems?'"

"What happened? Did they get to the client's place on time?" John asked eagerly.

The old man paused for a moment. "You know, I never found out," Kip answered with a smile. "What's important here is Alan's moment of discovery and enlightenment. He realized that what people root for is sometimes in conflict with their own best interest and the interest of the team."

John was silent. The story of Alan and Peter affected him because he could see there had been a few times when he too had not rooted for his team's success, especially when he'd felt slighted. Was he a Dissident, then? He started going over the four Dominant Traits in his mind. No, he concluded, he *couldn't* be a Dissident. The role of the Hero—helping, encouraging, championing others —clearly attracted him the most. And he remem-

96

bered Kip's comments that becoming a Hero was a never-ending process. He felt he had a long way to go. Suddenly, he had new insight, and with it, new questions.

"Kip, you keep talking about each of us having a *Dominant* Trait. Does this mean that we have other traits as well? As I think about my experiences, I can see that I have acted in all four capacities at one time or another."

"You know, John, you have a great deal of insight for someone so young," Kip responded respectfully. "You are right, of course. No one's behavior is one-dimensional. In fact, have you ever noticed how many roles you play in a day? For example, when you return routine phone calls, you may be acting like any of thousands of 9 to 5ers. An hour later you may be backing a new proposal presented by an unpopular person solely because you see its merit. At that moment you are acting like a Hero. . . ."

"I see what you mean. During one work day I may be changing roles several times, using different traits."

97

"Right. And yet, for each of us there is a Dominant Trait that defines our personality most of the time. But as the situation dictates, each of us may switch roles."

John nodded in understanding, but he wasn't yet satisfied. "Kip, we talked about Dissidents, and we agree that they should be made to feel part of the team again, or that they need to have an insight into their own behavior. But what happens if, as happened to me, you have an employee who is so bent on the righteousness of his cause that he deliberately sabotages the organization's efforts?"

"Then you may have on your hands a more complex and dangerous situation," Kip answered gravely. "You may have encountered the type I call the **Terrorist**."

John's eyes widened as Kip continued in a low voice. "There are some people, and they are very few, who can never see themselves as part of the team. The reasons are complex, ranging from lack of family identification as children to a sense of quiet superiority to the group. It's not a healthy psychological state."

"Are they Terrorists because they don't want to fit in?"

"No, they are Terrorists because of their behavior. For example, they may be computer programmers who introduce a faulty program —they call it *computer virus*—just to destroy the work of others. Or they may engage in industrial espionage. They rationalize their behavior by creating in their minds wrongs and injustices that don't exist."

"Are there many Terrorists in a typical organization?"

"Fortunately, Terrorists are pretty rare. But their destructive ability far exceeds their number."

John let out a low whistle.

Kip continued. "Great care must be taken before labeling someone a Terrorist. In fact, if you aren't careful with your labels you could get yourself into a heap of trouble. Only extreme behavior would ever fall into this category."

"What do you do when you're absolutely positive that someone is a Terrorist?" inquired John.

"If I were absolutely convinced that someone was acting in a way that was causing the organization definite harm, I would have to move for that person's dismissal. But again, you must be very careful to document your case with facts and not suspicions."

"Kip, you seem so careful in talking about Terrorist behavior. Why?"

"Because too often in autocratic organizations people use labels to unjustly crucify their enemies. If I'm reluctant to talk about this issue it's because I'm sensitive to the injustice people suffered because of their background or politics. Even in America we had to deal with the McCarthy era hysteria. People in an organization can also get paranoid and start labeling anyone who disagrees with the authorities as Terrorists. So please, be careful with this," Kip concluded emphatically.

John looked at his watch. It was almost 10:30.

"We'll be in Kansas City soon," Kip said with

barely disguised excitement.

It took a moment before John realized that Kansas City was where he was to meet Peggy Bentley, Kip's goddaughter and the California Zephyr's chief engineer for the next shift.

◆

The train screeched to a halt, and the loudspeaker blared their arrival in Kansas City. Kip turned to John. "Better take your overcoat if you'd like to join me. We'll have to get off the train and walk to the front to reach the engineer's compartment."

John inhaled the bracing air as they exited their car. It felt good, although the contrast to his warm compartment was a shock to his senses. The terminal was unusually busy for that time of night, with lots of sleepy children in the arms of their parents. John followed Kip, who was walking briskly through the scattered crowds. In spite of his years, Kip had the bouyant gait of someone half his age.

When they finally reached the engine, Kip called to Peggy, who was just about to embark. They greeted each other affectionately.

John waited for the two to catch up on family news. Shortly after, Kip turned around and introduced them to each other.

Peggy was an energetic woman in her mid-thirties, with intelligent eyes and a friendly yet professional manner. As she shook hands with John, Kip recounted to Peggy the topic of their conversation.

Peggy smiled a smile of recognition. "So what do you think of the Heroic Environment?"

"I think it's the most important concept I've ever heard," John replied quietly but firmly.

Peggy's face turned serious. "Well, they certainly don't teach these kinds of ideas in school. But I know they work."

"How?" asked John.

"Because Kip helped my father institute the

concepts in his business, and they have been a guiding light for him and, incidentally, for our entire family ever since."

"What made you decide to become a railroad engineer ... I mean, it's not the typical career ...."

"You mean for a woman, don't you?" Peggy said, laughing. "I'm afraid Kip is responsible for that, too. I've always loved trains, and Kip encouraged me to pursue my dream, even though it was unconventional."

"So now that you've achieved your goal ..."

"I haven't achieved my goal," interrupted Peggy. My goal is to bring back rail travel as a major way of transporting people. We're a long way from that, and yet our highways are becoming more and more crowded and our air more polluted. But I'm gratified to see how many people are coming back to train travel. One day, I hope we'll use it here as much as it is used in other developed countries like Japan, France, and West Germany."

"And how do you propose to achieve this?" John asked, fascinated.

"I want to keep reinforcing the progress we're making by helping institute the Heroic Environment here. And to do this properly, I hope one day to become a leader and spokesperson for the rail industry."

"Wow, you certainly know what you want," John said, a bit enviously.

"Don't you, John?"

"I'm still working on it," confided the young man, suddenly feeling like a high school freshman.

Kip, who had been listening to the exchange with keen interest, jumped in. "I have no doubts that John will make important contributions. But for now, we all must board the train."

For the first time, John noticed that he was tired. It had been a long and exciting day. After saying their goodbyes to Peggy, Kip and John returned to their compartment. Their bunks had been turned down for the night. Both agreed to continue their discussion in the morning.

Chapter 6

The Role
of the
Navigator
in the
Heroic
Environment

The following morning, as they sat down for breakfast, John looked at Kip thoughtfully. He was excited about seeing his family in less than two hours, especially his little Lauren. Yet he was also reluctant to see this journey end. He had learned so much, and still he felt as if he had opened the door only a crack. He did feel confident, however, that what he had learned would serve as a guiding light for the rest of his career. Now he felt that he had new meaning and purpose. Wherever he ended up working, he would strive to implement the Heroic Environment.

Kip was taking a long sip of coffee when John

addressed him. "Before our journey together ends, are there any more important areas we should cover?" he asked.

The older man thought for a moment. "Let's talk about change," he said, putting down his cup. Perhaps one of the most important things to understand is the tremendous speed in which change occurs today. It might even be more accurate to say that change occurs *continuously*. This is especially true in business, where changes in global economic conditions, technology, consumer preferences, and so forth can cause loss of business or unearth new opportunities almost overnight. The problem is that most organizations aren't set up to notice and react to change quickly enough."

"I guess you're right. People do talk about this a lot nowadays," John said, sounding less than convinced. "But aren't there still many old-style companies that keep making a profit year in and year out?"

"Not really," said Kip. "That's a common misconception. By 1970 more than half the Fortune 500 companies of 1950 were eaten up by mergers or shut their doors for lack of profitability. Today, fewer still are in business."

"Why?"

"There are many reasons why this happened," said Kip, "but there is one common thread: Most of these companies lacked the process to accept and benefit from new information and to make the appropriate course corrections. Without the ability to anticipate future trends and needs, these organizations lost their way."

"I think I understand," John said, still unconvinced, "but can you give me an example of this?"

Kip thought for a moment, and then his eyes brightened. "John, imagine a ship traveling in a stormy sea. The captain tells the crew, 'Keep going straight forward. I don't know what's ahead, but that's how we've always traveled.'"

"That would mean certain disaster," said John, who knew something about sailing. "The captain would run the ship aground, or worse. You can't maneuver a ship in stormy seas without a navigator."

"Exactly," said Kip, smiling with satisfaction. "The trouble with many companies is that they expect their leader to act as both captain and **Navigator**. These two roles require two separate abilities that seldom exist in any one individual."

"So who should be the Navigators in a business?" asked John.

"People at the forefront in every aspect of the business. These may include the salespeople who are on the front line dealing with customers and competitors, the scientists and engineers who are aware of technological breakthroughs, your marketing people, warehouse personnel, and anyone else who is in a position to notice change. All these people are crucial because they can read danger signals and convey advance information long before management would ever find out."

"This makes sense, of course," said John. "But doesn't management usually get this kind of information anyway?"

"Not in most organizations. The irony is that top managers *think* they get the straight scoop.

What they get instead is *filtered information*."

John looked perplexed, so Kip continued.

"*Filtered information* is information that has been screened before it's sent upstairs. Think of it this way. Let's suppose you saw a trend that could negatively affect the future of your company, but you also knew that your concerns would challenge the most cherished beliefs of your CEO and his immediate staff. You've been around this company long enough to know that your warnings would be rejected and might even put your career at risk. Would you send your data upstairs?"

"I don't know. But if I did, I'd phrase my concerns in such a way that they might have a chance to survive."

"Then you'd be sending *filtered information* upstairs—a diluted version of your strong warnings. Now, your leaders would *assume* that they were receiving the straight stuff. And herein lies the distortion.

"Autocratic environments that view the very

113

existence of contrary and dissenting information as threatening and destabilizing are inflexible and therefore brittle. Because all they deal with is *filtered information*, they are unable to perceive change quickly. As a result, they will always lose market share to companies that encourage comments and insights from every member of the team."

Now John was beginning to really understand the full meaning of what he was hearing.

"What I am inferring from all this, Kip, is that unlike autocratic organizations which are slow to respond to change, the Heroic Environment, which encourages everyone to act as Navigators, is much more flexible and responsive to change."

Kip nodded approvingly. "Autocratic managers feel comfortable only when they hear ideas and information that confirm their previously formed assumptions. In contrast, Heroic managers worry when they haven't considered all possible options."

Kip went on. "In the autocratic organization, discipline and power form the glue that holds the organization together. The leadership has certain beliefs about how the world works, and they want to make sure everyone throughout the organization embraces these beliefs. This kind of rigidity may have worked during times of very slow change. Today, these beliefs create a 'Berlin Wall' of the mind, which halts vital information about the changing world."

"Okay, I've got it now," said John excitedly. "This is powerful stuff. But then tell me, Kip, what is management's role in this brave new world of constant change?"

Kip answered without hesitation. "Management's ultimate role is to *understand* the meaning of what its Navigators are reporting and *act* appropriately and courageously. The tough thing is that today's top managers have to trust others to notice the changes and recommend direction. Like the captain of a ship, management will then devise a strategy for the implementation of the changes its Navigators recommend.

"What happens if management simply uses the information supplied by others and forms its own interpretation of what changes to implement?"

"It's a halfway measure that can occasionally work. The problem is that management can easily fall victim to its own *perceptual bias*."

"Wait a minute," said John. "You just threw a new concept at me. Please explain."

"Sorry," said Kip, smiling. *"Perceptual bias* means that people see what they expect to see and ignore the rest."

"You mean like not seeing the car keys that are right under your nose instead of where you thought they were?" asked John.

"Right. Except that the consequences are much more serious in business. It can lead to a company designing the wrong product, entering a new market that it is unable to penetrate successfully, and so on. What's frightening about *perceptual bias* is that we don't know we have it—it's invisible. Unfortunately, its effects don't remain invisible for long."

116

"You can have all the right information, but if your bias affects what you see, you will still not act appropriately," confirmed John, as he took notes furiously.

Kip smiled, and continued.

"John, this is the essence of what I'm saying: Management's best strategy is to create a Heroic Environment that encourages its people to come up with insights about the changing market. Management's role is to implement those changes in the best way possible."

John remained silent for a few minutes as he digested the lesson he was learning. Finally, he said thoughtfully, "What you are asking management to do is trust others in the organization to set the course for its future and to focus on the execution of this direction. Boy, it seems like you're asking management to take a tremendous leap of faith."

"Yes, I am. But I'm afraid the alternative is a terminal case of going out of business or eventually being taken over," Kip said with finality.

117

It took John a moment or two to finish writing. Looking at his notebook, he said, "Kip, now that this trip is coming to an end, let me see if I can summarize the essence of what I've learned so far:

- Heroic Environments create a bond through which all people within an organization participate fully in its shared purpose, and they do it by creating a common language of internal and external values. Therefore, working toward the creation of a Heroic Environment is the first step.

- A Heroic Environment brings out the best in all positive personality types, and when confronted with someone who feels left out, it makes every effort to make that person feel like a members of the team.

- An organization can ensure its survival and success by understanding that market forces change continually, and it's up to the Navigators at all levels of the organization to send unfiltered information to management and to participate in choosing the right course for the future.

"I couldn't have said it as well," Kip said with genuine modesty.

Chapter 7

The
Beginning
of a
New Journey

As they were leaving the dining room, Kip looked at his watch and said, "We'll be arriving in Denver in forty minutes." John didn't answer. He was still torn between his great desire to see his family and regret that he was about to say goodbye to his mentor.

Suddenly, he realized that he hadn't asked Kip enough questions about himself. In a way, it all seemed so mysterious. Yet John felt a genuine sense of satisfaction about the mystery. It was as if the bond between them had been built purely around the nobility of the ideas they'd discussed.

Armed with these new concepts, John knew now that he would not change jobs. He would stay where he was and work to build a Heroic Environment.

After a long silence, John said, "Kip, I don't know how to thank you for what you've taught me."

Kip smiled and said, "You can thank me by letting me know how you're doing." And then, with special warmth, he added, "John, I think you know that I'm rooting for your success."

"Kip, will you be coming through Denver on one of your future trips?"

"Yes, I'll be passing through in April."

John's eyes lit up. "I'd be honored to have you stay with us."

"That's very kind of you," said Kip, smiling. The two men shook hands and exchanged business cards as the train slowed.

———◆———

After receiving a loving homecoming greeting from his wife Cathy and his little girl Lauren, John and his family hurried away from the platform. Suddenly, he heard his name called. As he turned around, he was surprised to see the president of his company and one of the vice presidents.

"Mr. Williams," he exclaimed with surprise, "what are you doing here?"

"We were in Denver for a meeting at your plant when this blasted snowstorm closed the airport, so the corporate jet is useless. I have to be in Los Angeles in two days, so this is the only alternative."

John smiled. "It's not such a bad alternative, sir. It may take longer, but it's amazing the new perspective a train ride can give. Oh, by the way, where are you sitting?"

The president looked at his ticket. "Compartment 417-C."

Suppressing a smile, John responded simply, "Sir, when you get back to corporate headquarters, I'd like to call you. I believe there'll be a lot for us to talk about."

A Special Thanks

The information contained in this tale is a result of research begun 15 years ago at International Survey Research (ISR). **During that period over 2,400,000 workers in 40 countries**—senior managers, middle managers, supervisors, and staff personnel—from 30 different industries participated in numerous attitude and behavior studies on how they wanted to be treated. It is from these expressed needs that the Eight Principles of the Heroic Environment sprang.

A registered trademark for the Heroic Environment® and its process was granted to Heroic Environments, Inc. in 1990. Programs, workshops, tapes (audio & video), and workbooks are now available to assist organizations and companies to adopt and apply Heroic Principles. For further information contact:

Heroic Environment, Inc.
11811 Northeast First/Suite 207
Bellevue, Washington 98005

(800) 423-9327
(206) 453-0706
(206) 453-6012 FAX

127

Acknowledgments

One afternoon in October 1985, a freelance writer by the name of Roger Parker wandered into my office and asked, "What do you do around here?" Without thinking I said, "I help companies keep out of harm's way. I guess you could say that I perform corporate Heroics!"

From that brief exchange a friendship was born. For years I tried to understand where I belonged and where I could find *my* happiness. I came to realize that I was looking for my Heroic Environment. I started my search and quickly realized that a Heroic Environment is a workplace that everyone deserves.

In my search, I met many who extended their hands and hearts in helping me discover what a Heroic Environment is. I want to acknowledge those people who were part of my journey.

My wife Sharon's constant love and belief in the project made my efforts possible. Her thoughtful questions, direct approach, and wise counsel always came at the right time. I am forever grateful to Ben Dominitz, my editor, for his wisdom, humor, editing and writing skills, patience, and tenacity. To Mike Bell, a large debt is owed for his energy, enthusiasm, creativity, and uncanny ability to get the very best from me in my search; and to Jeff Goforth for his continued faith in the project. To Alan Zerkin, Richard Geller, Colin Haynes, Doug Glen, Pat McGovern, Dick Williams, Judith Briles, Mark Pastin, Joe Lipson, Richard Leeds, and Jack Stanek, a thank you, for they seemed to be there at just the right time. To Bill Gladstone, who first understood the power of creating a Heroic Environment, a debt of gratitude is owed. To John Mitzel and Marlen Bell, who believed so strongly in the concept that they brought the Heroic Environment Program into their organization before it was ready and became our first client, thank you for taking the risk for your organization's sake. To Ruth and Joe, my mother and father, who patiently read and commented on the many rewrites and continued to love me in spite of it, thank you. And thanks to the hundreds of people who mercifully listened to the Heroic Environment ideas in their early stages.

Acknowledgments

Finally, to Stanley Kiplinger (Kip) whose wisdom, patience, and gentle mentoring allowed this story to be told, a special thanks. And, oh yes, thanks to the stranger who whispered in my ear, "There are no accidents."

131